First Frost

FIRST FROST

Poems by Kathryn Kerr
Photographs by Raymond Bial

STORMLINE PRESS
URBANA ILLINOIS
1985

Library of Congress Catalog Card Number: 85-090425

International Standard Book Number: 0-935153-00-4

Stormline Press, Inc., a non-profit service organization, publishes works of literary and artistic distinction by Illinois writers and artists.

Stormline Press, Inc.
Post Office Box 593
Urbana, Illinois 61801
Manufactured in the United States of America.

ACKNOWLEDGMENTS

Publication of this book has been made possible in part by a grant from the Illinois Arts Council and a Grassroots Regrant from the Arts Council of Champaign County. Kathryn Kerr received an Illinois Arts Council Fellowship for the completion of the manuscript.

We would like to thank Linda LaPuma Bial and Michael Spooner for their diligence and insight in editing the poems and arranging the photographs.

A number of the poems in *First Frost* previously appeared in *Coneflower, Great River Review, Jump River Review, Matrix, Mississippi Valley Review,* and *Spoon River Quarterly.*

PREFACE

The Midwest has often been described as a "region in which life goes on elsewhere." Midwesterners are led to believe that art also occurs in other (usually distant) places. However, the artists from other areas often portray people living on farms and in small towns as stereotypical characters ranging from the sentimental to the bumpkinesque. At best farm life is viewed romantically in terms of the "good life." Unfortunately artists with the experience and ability to deal honestly with rural and small town themes are seldom encouraged and often ignored altogether.

Stormline Press was established in early 1985 to publish and otherwise assist writers and artists whose work sensitively and accurately portrays rural life. I hope *First Frost* and other publications of the press will also lead to a greater understanding and appreciation of the realities of rural culture.

Through her poetry Kathryn Kerr speaks convincingly of childhood and coming of age on a farm near Buncombe, a small town located deep in the woods and fields of southern Illinois. Having spent a good portion of my own childhood on farms and in small towns in Indiana, Michigan, and Illinois, I suppose I am most struck by the authenticity of Kathryn's poetry. I consider it rare to find a poet in America with the combination of talent and background to write meaningfully of rural and small town life, in this case from a woman's unique perspective.

As a photographer I have been working along themes similar to Kathryn's for the past fourteen years and I have known Kathryn for nearly as long. So, when the idea arose to combine poetic and photographic vision in a book we were naturally enthused by the possibilities.

Admittedly such an undertaking involves elements of risk. The work must dovetail so that both art forms are strengthened. In order to achieve a pleasing balance we have spent a great deal of time selecting and arranging poems and photographs. The result, I believe, is a unique and effective debut publication of Stormline Press.

Raymond Bial
September 1985

CONTENTS

INTRODUCTION

What's a transplanted city boy like me doing writing an introduction to a collection of rural poems and photos? Well, I met Kathryn Kerr about eight years ago at the Monday night read-and-critique sessions of the Red Herring Poets at the University of Illinois, and she must have known from my comments that I was drawn to the rich interiors of her poetry about the life and landscape of the rural Midwest.

It took considerably longer to move from an appreciation of her precise, insightful art to a feeling for the sprawling prairie itself. But the transformation came, about two years ago. I am always suspicious of other people's epiphanies, but I swear that two of them have happened to me. The first was when I was about 17, riding the Desire streetcar up Royal Street in the French Quarter in New Orleans. I had lived in the city all my life and had always considered the Quarter a dirty, ugly place. So as we stopped at Dumaine Street, I wasn't prepared to glance casually out the window and be stunned by the arrangement of wrought iron grillwork, buildings of incredible tone and character, and people threading their way comfortably through the scene. Since then, the Quarter (even the repainted Quarter of 1985) has never failed to move me with its dark, brooding beauty.

The second transformation was in 1983, when I got so tired of the unrelieved flatness of corn and soybean fields surrounding Champaign–Urbana that I wrote an altogether unpleasant poem about it. The Red Herring Poets allowed it was pretty good verse, but I was embarrassed to be so annoyed at the environment that seemed to nourish them. Not long after, I was driving at dusk toward Rantoul along the endless horizon of Highway 57, and *poof*, the warty little farmhouses and barns and silos looked and felt different than before. So did the greywhite sky, revealing itself suddenly as a canopy of limitless – though subtle – variety. I thought of Kathryn's poetry and felt like the kid who memorized a lot of stuff in the 7th grade but didn't begin to understand it until years later. I think now that my own poem was a kind of purgation, freeing me to learn how to love what natives have long found lovable among Midwestern corn rows.

There's a great deal to love in the poems and photographs of *First Frost*. Like Annie Dillard, Kathryn Kerr has a gift for exploring the relationships between nature and everyday people without sentimentalizing them. Overwhelmingly, her affection for her subjects comes through; but in pieces like "Squirrels" and "Rust," she acknowledges simple horrors woven into the simple life. The complexity of family relationships and tender adolescent longings are revealed in "Wolves," "Owls," and "American Bandstand." There's humor, too, in poems like "Pauline Bites Her Thread in Two" and in the perfect country cadences of "Miss Stoner's Story."

Ray Bial's marvelous photos are something else. That is to say, they are in no sense "illustrations" of Kathryn's poetry. Rather, the poems and pictures complement each other. Clusters of each reflect the spirit and sense of rural life, expanding our understanding though different media.

I find the selection of Ray's works here even more affecting than those in his well-reviewed book *Ivesdale*, (Champaign County Historical Archives, 1982). Released from the essentially programmatic demands of the earlier book, Ray has gathered images that are, to my eyes at least, more intensely rural in content and more universal in appeal. His works and Kathryn Kerr's splendidly illustrate Hamlin Garland's contention that provincialism is the truest source of genuine culture.

Charles Suhor
National Council of Teachers of English
Urbana, Illinois, 1985

DOWN HOME
– for Rod

When the sun came up,
we fed the hogs
then crossed the pasture
with the dog.
It was hot at 6 a.m.,
and we were tired.

Home,
to smell the damp
woods in the ravine,
clover in the sun.
We honored the years
it took to turn

poor soil into cedar.
Seven barns and sheds,
we went in every one,
examined each post
each trimmed and notched
and fitted by hand.

The walls and roofs
are salvage.
You are proud
to waste nothing,
need little,
to farm.

SERMON

When Grandpa followed
a horse-drawn plough,
he was up at dawn.
With a few quick words
to his wife and sons,
he went away with a bucket
of cornbread and ham
and a jug of milk for noon.
The shape of the clouds
and rhythm of hooves
told him all he needed.
Evenings, a few phrases
told the whole day.
On Sunday his sermon
was a well-adjusted,
smoothed and polished
planting tool.

EARLY SUNDAY

Hard as hens' beaks Grandma's thumbs pushed
clumps of corn from the cob. As it fell golden in the dust
the hens gathered around gossiping, stretching their
necks, yellow bills pecking around her shoes. She let the
red cob slip empty through her fingers, grasped the grey
Dominecker neck and swung the hen in circles in the
purple morning sky. The hens scattered scolding while
the one landed headless, kicking and flapping her wings
in the grass. Slowly she wound down, each flap, kick,
and squirt of blood less until she was just a tremble.
Handing me the head, Grandma grabbed the yellow
legs, took it to the iron kettle of boiling water and
plunged it in. She stood silently pulling off clumps of
wet feathers. I caressed the down around the comb and
golden eye. The hens went back to finish the corn.

9

SQUIRRELS

Jim held one up by the loose back and I sliced through, then slipped the knife around the waist. He held the arms while I pulled the pants down to the little claw feet and cut them off. We tried to pull the tail out, but it usually broke.

Patiently the dog chewed the pants while we slipped the sweater up over the head, trimming the ears and leaving the squirrel big-eyed and grinning.

Still Jim held him while I put the knife in the V of the ribs and opened the warm blue belly down to the stub of the tail. The entrails burst out purple for the waiting dog. I cut them free, then opened the ribs for the heart and lungs.

With the knife tip, I popped the eyes out. Thumb against the blade edge got the last black whiskers. We put him in the refrigerator.

In the oven there were biscuits still in the pan and soft, cold bacon stuck to the bottom of the pale blue pie pan. From the dark pantry we got a purple pint jar of jelly.

We cut each biscuit in two, spooned jelly on each half, stuck in a piece of bacon, and washed it down with warm milk.

We took the last few biscuits out on the back steps and threw them one at a time to the dog. He caught each one in its arc and swallowed it whole. Then with whiskers curved against the dish, his tongue whispered it clean.

Touch

Mother was a washcloth
smearing my face clean,
shoes tied to last all day,
the back of the hairbrush
on top of my head
if I wiggled
when it pulled.

Father was a knuckle
on my head at dinner time,
a snowball on the side of my face,
the force that lifted
me by one arm
while the yardstick
set me straight.

First Frost

Always there was one evening when we'd get home and Mom would say, "You kids come to the garden with me. It's supposed to frost tonight," and we'd put on patched jeans and work jackets and old shoes shaped like our feet.

We'd leave the steam of supper hanging and go out where the crickets played and the air smelled like leaves. While we weren't looking, the garden had gotten pale and lank. Tomato plants sprawled drunkenly as we picked their pockets of red, then orange, then yellow, before we turned to the squash and took everything as big as a fist. Then we kidnapped little cucumbers that stuck our fingers, and peppers, the soft, red, wrinkled old dwarves.

When the baskets and buckets were put on the porch with the apples, I'd go to the grape row and find the last bruised recluses under the leaves.

The sky was a memory of sun, swallows swept into the barn where the zing zing of milk filled the bucket. When the sound was almost a whisper, Dad would slap the cow's flank and come out with the bucket in one hand, the other out at an angle, and within a minute of him slamming the screen door, I'd hear Mom yell, "*Kath*-ryn, come wash for *sup*-per."

BUTTER

It turns in my stomach,
turns like the paddle
of the square churn
that sat uncomfortably
cornered between my thighs.
As I turned and turned
the crank handle
the gears whirred.
I heard the scrape
of the nails of puppies
our neighbor packed
new-born into her churn
before she filled it
with water.

CELLAR

Strong as mildew or wet leaves
the cellar smell came warm.
Each step down darkened
as the door closed.
We flashed a cone of light
across damp space.
Smells of apples and pumpkins
sorted themselves from potatoes.

Peaches under blue glass,
pale as dead fish, waited,
dark bloody beets beside them.
Pint jars of jam bordered
blocks of green beans;
a quilt pattern pieced
with shelves of wood.

Baskets full, we turned to see
the harvestmen huddled by the door,
keepers of the cellar's warmth.
Each eye reflected red.

WOLVES

Like a she-wolf,
that mother of mine
gave just enough milk
to keep me alive
and hungry.
Don't cry.
Indian children
bound to cradle boards
couldn't cry
or the wolves
would find them.
In my narrow bed
I cried silent all night
for she wouldn't say
the wolves couldn't get me.
Those caged cries,
like wolves,
were never tamed.
On dark nights
they pursue me,
leap at my throat
and gnaw at my stomach.

Rat

The child sat silent, sleepy; food on her hands and face. The man set the cup on the table, leaned the chair back against the kitchen wall, put his hands on the gun that lay across his legs. The woman untied the apron, untied the bib, said, "Don't shoot in here, you'll scare her." He said, "You want it to sleep with her?"

Eggs

Over coffee he said, "They're barnloft eggs. Don't know how long a broody hen's been up there. Didn't know one was missing when I fed." Beside the cookstove the warm eggs sat small and freckled in a rusty coffee can; a bit of hay in the bottom to cushion.

While rice simmered, she washed up, broke one egg into a chipped blue saucer, then called the girl to come and look. From the bright yolk, a web of blood lines tangled. The heart beat; a tremble. She pointed to the eye, the beak, the little feet, where the wing would be. The tremble weakened, slowed, stopped. She emptied it into the slop-bucket, cracked another egg into the saucer saying, "I'm glad I didn't break that one into the pudding."

CISTERN

Near the end of the August dry spell, the bucket
started scraping, coming up half-filled, murky and
smelly. He brought a barrel from his father's well and set
it on the porch.

Bucket after bucket he drew from the cistern and
threw on the flowers and garden. In one splash was the
white sack skin of a toad.

In green rubber boots he stepped careful on the
ladder tied to the tile, then hands and feet wedged on
down the laid stones cool to the bottom. The child's face
silhouetted smaller and smaller in the shrinking circle
of sky.

With the spade he scraped the bottom, sounds filled
the walls. Soot, leaves, and formless objects filled the
bucket. His wife pulled each load up exclaiming.

He finished with the broom, then rags, wedged his
way up the stones slippery-footed to the ladder his wife
assured him was firm.

In noon sun he pulled off the boots, drank a dipperful
from the barrel, searched the sky for clouds.

Miss Stoner's Story

Be careful with that big knife, Sweetheart,
and watch how you push back those leaves.
Big old snake lay up there in the shade,
bite right through those little cloth shoes.

Cut these big stalks down at the ground,
now. You ever hear of a body bit by a snake
and the snake died? It's God's Truth,
but I wouldn't a'believed it.

In '45, I recall, the boys was at war
and I's helping Mamma with this rhubarb.
Old Copperhead laying up under the leaves
and it still early morning. A hot day.

Well, I didn't see him till he struck.
Here, Honey, don't take that stalk
and it all wormy. But my old arm's so tough
his teeth slid over to the loose skin.

He caught the hide, here, like this.
Bit clean through and stuck his own lip.
Fastened on me like a mole trap.
Had a time prizing him loose.

He thrashed around that furrow
biting his own tail. Died after noon.
You know a snake can poison hisself?
Even the dogs wouldn't touch him.

Can you tote this bag full?
Walk at the edge of the road, now.
Cars drop over that hill real fast.
Come back when gooseberries are ready.

53

EVOLUTION

Preacher Taylor had no training
and no church, just the calling;
so he saved people in cornfields
at harvest time, led prayers
at reunions and threshing dinners,
spoke at foot-washings, funerals, and baptisms.
Couples too young to marry
without their parents' blessing
(but sometimes in the family way)
could go to Preacher's house after supper.
He'd bless their hasty union
there in the parlor.

The parlor had a high-backed horse-hair sofa
with wooden carving every edge, back, side.
My child fingers followed those trenches
digging the dust out till Mother said
"Now you sit still." And I sat, feet straight out
turning them, both in, both out
until Aunt Ellie, Preacher's wife,
would take me to the kitchen.

Aunt Ellie was about my size
when I was ten, her thin hair
bunned like a head of Queen Anne's
Lace above her hunch back.
But she had her ways of dealing.
Made her son one day, he was twenty,
bring her foot-stool from the bedroom.
She stepped up, slapped him soundly
one side the face, then the other,
said that'd teach him to sass *her*.
Made him put her stool away.

On the back porch by the kitchen
hung overalls, brand-new
but split between the seams
and down both legs, little holes
punched here and there
in the stiff, dark, unwashed fabric.
Combine got Preacher's pants-leg one day.
He threw himself down to pray,
and the Lord let the new pants
rip right off the old man.
He walked through broad daylight fields
giving thanks in just his shirt-tails.

At the end of Preacher's front porch
was a fossil, scales reptilian and cool
to my bare feet. He thought it was a lizard.
an alligator, maybe, a big fish;
oval chunk about two feet through.
At college I learned it was *Lepididendron*,
a fern tree of the Carboniferous.
But it was too late to ask the Preacher
his views on evolution.

BURNING

Preacher Taylor every spring
set fire to broom-sage in his pasture.
One of the great-grandkids
would run up breathless,
"Can Harry   please come
Granddad's fire   done got away."
Dad and some neighbors would save
the old man's wooden fences,
his barn and haystack.
Mom said someday the old fool
would have a heart attack
burning his fields like that.

The biology teacher said burning
was poor conservation,
wasted humus, started erosion.
Charles Taylor said his people
burned their fields for eighty years
and never had to spray.

Phelpses had a dinner bell,
rang it at noon, summertimes.
Told us ever we heard it
any other time, come running.
It meant fire, disaster.
Sharon Phelps said neighbors' buckets
had saved their cousin's home.
They had a pond nearby.
Cummingses had a bell
and Boners, and the same signal.
I wanted us to have one.

"By the time somebody went to town
  and phoned the firetruck from Cypress,
  we'd be like the church
  at Pleasant Grove," Mom said,
"all burned but the bell
  when the truck got there,
  then had to pay for it
  driving out of its district."
  Prevention was my mother's way.

BRUSH

It stood on Mother's dresser, black and white, a penguin on a wooden floe. Below were long, soft bristles for brushing lapels. We put it on a fence post and shot it off again and again. It fell head first into dead grass. When we picked it up, the bristles were soft to our hands and cheeks, the penguin smooth and cold.

Next day I took the gun behind the smokehouse and shot a sparrow in the cherry tree. It fell once. Soft warm feathers smelled like my brother's hair. The feet were small, flexible, and cold.

MESMERIZED

My sister charmed a serpent, told us she had ridden
with a snake on the tricycle, had pedaled around turned
porch posts, holding the wheels, just so, missing the
edges, looking dizzy into irises below.

We didn't believe her, told her to look at a book, play
dolls, She rode again, stretching for the pedals, singing
songs from Sunday School rewoven as her own. The
snake's head hung copper between pink heels. In shadow
of wheels, spokes, pedals, posts, elliptical eyes shown.
Mother saw her finish the ride, saw it let its body slide
from beneath the seat and slip, quick as slamming the
screen door, over porch planks rough-edged as screams.

MERCIFUL

At the sound of the shot, Johnny made footprints fast across the frosted grass to the downed pig. His knife flashed ice as he lifted the head. Then there was red on the blade, the hands, the frost, and rising steam. From a hole between the eyes, blood trickled to the ringed nostrils. Blue eyes slowly turned up into lashed lids. Ears lay soft and loose against denim sleeves. "That Johnny," Dad said, "He doesn't even give them a chance to squeal."

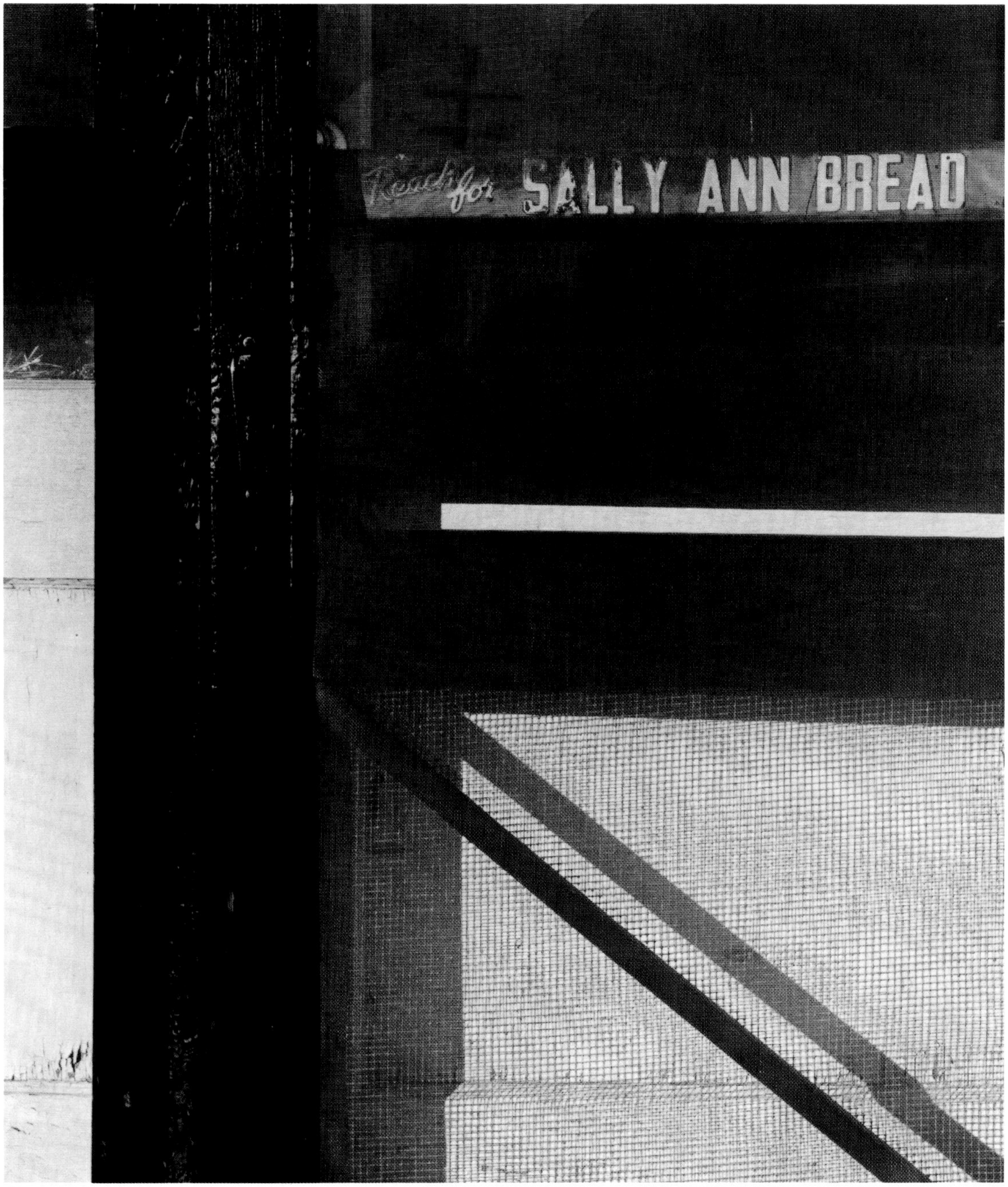
Reach for SALLY ANN BREAD

Owls

Afternoon's faint warmth was fading when a silent form settled soft in the oak above. After a moment, a low syllable. Another folded wide wings, settling in the next treetop. Another note and they sat silent, swaying with wind in the lowering dark. They tried several trees, chose open limbs, discussed them in hoarse almost-whispers. They mated then against the dark blue sky, huge feathers flapping quiet; parted, shook themselves, and flew together toward the ice-edged creek, calling nine low notes over and over.

Frozen on stones and roots below, she breathed slow, hearing only her heart. She rush stumbled up the faint cattle path through the open woods to the orchard and the house beyond. Slowly she opened the kitchen, entered with her face turned. They sat with papers spread over the table. Mother spoke, waited for her to hang her coat and leave the room. She went to the back bedroom and stood in the cold looking out the dark west window toward the creek. Holding herself, she knew something new no one had told her.

Rust

She leaned her hot head
against the bus window,
watched the sun set rust-red
over fallow fields
orange with orchard grass
wet in the March wind.
She ached to be alone,
to be gone, to be grown.
Her chest had a catch
that kept her breathing.
Her belly hurt.
Underwear bound her,
it seemed, everywhere.

She was caught at home
in the heat of the kitchen.
Mom said, "Charlie Grider
turned over that old tractor
today." She saw his chest
crushed by the steering wheel,
rust on his leather vest.
His pipe was broken. He had
a little blood in his mouth.
"We've got to go
to the funeral home.
You can stay here
and study if you want."

When she undressed
there was rust in her pants.
Chilled, she remembered
long orange grass blown
waves over green shoots
on drenched hillsides.
Remembered the moustache
of the man who died
with blood in his mouth.

PAULINE BITES HER THREAD IN TWO, THEN SAYS:

First I ever learned about sex
was from an old medical text:
Problems in Obstetrics.
Every misformed pelvis possible
was pictured there.
Hemmorhoids, hernia, hydrocephalus –
you got it – tumors, twin pipes . . .
I married late. Worked a month waitressing
right after the wedding. Chili-mac
was the cheapest thing on the menu –
you know, beans and runny sauce
over spaghetti noodles.
Only serving I ever saw
came back. Came back up, that is,
on the old wino who laid his face
down in it before he left.
For a dollar an hour and tips
I cleaned it up,
fearing I'd have syphillis
from touching his "bodily fluids."
And since he'd left without paying,
the cashier took the tip.

AMERICAN BANDSTAND

Sandi and I sat sipping lemonade, watching American Bandstand from the damp fat folds of ourselves. The pretty thin blond demurely admitted that she shampooed her hair every day with Pamper. Dick approved. We thought of every day drawing the extra water with a bucket from the well. Thought of every day boiling water in the fly-buzz steamy kitchen, thought of the second kettle boiling while we were head down in the dishpan, lathered-up. We thought of the vinegar rinse, of spending half of each day in curlers till our hair almost dried in the humidity. We thought of the cost of all those bottles of shampoo subtracted from the dollar we got each week if we were good. We got out another box of cookies.

AUNT ROSE REFERS OBLIQUELY TO HER SPINSTERHOOD

I had forgotten snow drifted
high as telphone poles
some winters, but the old photos
show it that way. No wonder
Cap wrote he wanted to marry.

Soil drifted like snow
those dust bowl summers. Oats
uprooted soon after sprouting.
Nothing seemed fastened.

He raised step-sisters,
then had no one. I heard
he died a drifter. No reason
I ever understood for drought
and the way things blow loose.

THANKSGIVING

Four o'clock flakes/ large and grey as feathers./ She walked from window to window,/ looked out and down the hill/ to the swollen creek.

She was sharp with the child,/ then turned tender./ The little girl held/ back from both.

Windows frosted feathery from the edges./ She put logs on the fire,/ kettles on the stove,/ music on the radio.

Evening turned lavender,/ then dark./ The trees began to move and talk.

She put on her coat,/ a pair of his boots,/ walked out to the edge of the hill./ Her own voice came/ back in the wind./ She went in./ The child lay on the hearth,/ eyes fixed on the fire./ She made her sit in a chair.

In silence they sat for a while./ Wind slammed the door./ She ran to the clock in the kitchen,/ began to pace again.

When he came, she scolded,/ then wept, then laughed/ as he pulled duck after duck/ from the sacks/ and jacket pockets.

By the fire they sat/ sipping, joking, plucking./ The child was wrapped in a quilt,/ allowed to sleep on the couch./ Wind rattled the windows./ They held fistfuls/ of feathers toward the flames./ Draft took the down,/ sent it light up the chimney,/ back into the wind/ and starless night.

Colophon

The photographs in this book were made on Ilford Pan F film and printed on Ilford Ilfobrom and Galerie papers by Raymond Bial.

The book was designed and the Bembo types set by Robert Chapdu of Four·C Typographers & Designers, Champaign Illinois.

The book was printed with photos in duotone on Warren Cameo Gloss paper by Andromeda Printing & Graphic Arts, Champaign Illinois.